America's Game
San Francisco Giants

Chris W. Sehnert

ABDO & Daughters
PUBLISHING

Published by Abdo & Daughters, 4940 Viking Dr., Suite 622, Edina, MN 55435.

Copyright ©1997 by Abdo Consulting Group, Inc., Pentagon Tower, P.O. Box 36036, Minneapolis, Minnesota 55435. International copyrights reserved in all countries. No part of this book may be reproduced in any form without written permission from the publisher. Printed in the United States.

Cover photo: Allsport
Interior photos: Wide World Photo, pages 1, 9, 11, 12, 14, 15, 16, 20,
                 21, 23, 27
                 Allsport, pages 5, 24

Edited by Paul Joseph

Library of Congress Cataloging–in–Publication Data

Sehnert, Chris W.
    San Francisco Giants / Chris W. Sehnert
        p. cm. — (America's game)
    Includes index.
    Summary: Discusses the history and notable players of the team that spent seventy-five years as the New York Giants and then moved to San Francisco after the 1957 season.
    ISBN 1-56239-683-8
    1. San Francisco Giants (Baseball team)—History—Juvenile literature. [1. San Francisco Giants (Baseball team)—History. 2. Baseball—History.] I. Title. II. Series.
GV875.S34S45 1997
796.357' 64' 0979461—dc20   96-17921
                                              CIP
                                              AC

Contents

San Francisco Giants

The Major League Baseball team known as the Giants has been playing "America's Game" since 1883. Their history begins in New York City, where for 75 years they played next to a plot of ground called Coogan's Bluff. In 1958, the Giants moved to San Francisco, California, where they have yet to win a World Championship.

The career of Willie Mays was split between New York's Polo Grounds and San Francisco's Candlestick Park. He is one of the many all-time great players who have worn the black and orange colors of the Giants. From Christy Mathewson to Barry Bonds, the rich tradition of Giants' baseball has carried on.

The Giants offer a window into the history of the game itself. The team has been involved in some of the most memorable and historic moments ever to take place on a diamond of dirt. Many have influenced the very way the game is played.

Facing page: Giants' Barry Bonds gets a hit during a game against the Colorado Rockies.

Gotham

In the early 1840s, the parks of New York City were occupied by groups of people playing various forms of an English game called "rounders." A men's club, known as the New York Knickerbockers, wrote down the rules to their version of the game, and called it "base ball." For this reason, "Gotham City" is known as the birthplace of America's National Pastime.

The New York Metropolitans and New York Gothams began play in 1883 on adjacent fields at the north end of Manhattan's Central Park. Their home fields were separated by canvas, and were built on grounds formerly used for polo. In 1884, the Metropolitans faced the Providence Grays in baseball's first World Series!

Jim Mutrie managed the Metropolitans to their American Association (AA) Pennant in 1884. The next season, Mutrie took over as manager of the National League (NL) Gothams. Looking at the size of his new lineup, "Truthful Jim" began calling the club "My Giants." The nickname stuck, and the New York Giants soon became contenders.

The Giants' roster included six players who would eventually be enshrined into the Baseball Hall of Fame. Mickey Welch and Tim Keefe combined to give New York the best pitching staff in baseball. Roger Connor led the NL with a .371 batting average in 1885, and was the most prolific home run hitter of the 19th century. Together with "Orator Jim" O'Rourke, John Montgomery Ward, and William "Buck" Ewing, the six were among the greatest players of their era. They brought New York two consecutive World Championships in 1888 and 1889.

With five of their top six players gone to the Players League (PL) in 1890, New York dropped to sixth place in the NL. Mickey Welch stayed with the team and was joined on the Giants' pitching staff by the incredible Amos Rusie. "The Hoosier Thunderbolt" would have a lasting effect on the game of baseball.

Rusie's fastball was legendary. He led the NL in shutouts in 1890 with 341, and again in 1891 with 337. The unhittable nature of Amos Rusie's heater was given as the reason for lengthening the pitching distance from 50 feet to 60 feet, 6 inches in 1893. Under the new rules, Amos led the league in strikeouts three more times in a row, from 1893 to 1895.

In 1894, New York finished second in the NL. Because the AA was no longer a major league, the NL's first- and second-place finishers faced off in the postseason. The Giants defeated the Baltimore Orioles in the first such series, known as the Temple Cup.

The New York Giants brought 3 World Championships to Gotham City in their first 12 seasons. In 1891, they moved into a new stadium built for the defunct PL. The new Polo Grounds would remain the home of Giants baseball for 67 years. Amos Rusie now shares space with Tim Keefe, John Ward, Mickey Welch, Buck Ewing, Jim O'Rourke, and Roger Connor in the Baseball Hall of Fame.

Big Six

The New York Giants traded Amos Rusie to the Cincinnati Reds in 1900. The fireballing veteran never won another major league contest. In exchange for Rusie, the Giants received Christy Mathewson.

Mathewson's fastball went by hitters with such speed that New York reporters nicknamed him "Big Six," after a local fire engine. Using his famous "fadeaway" screwball, Mathewson led the NL in shutouts and ERA five times.

Mathewson went on to pitch 17 seasons for New York, and compiled more wins (373) than any pitcher in NL history. He also recorded more 20-win seasons (12) than any pitcher in NL history. In 4 of those seasons, he picked up at least 30 wins.

When the Baseball Hall of Fame was established in 1936, it elected five players as the first to be immortalized. The list included Babe Ruth, Honus Wagner, Ty Cobb, Walter Johnson, and Christy Mathewson. Arriving first was not an unusual occurrence for "Big Six."

The turn of the century brought changes to Major League Baseball. In 1901, the American League (AL) established itself as a separate but equal partner to the "Senior Circuit." Two years later, a new round of World Series competition began.

John McGraw became the manager of the Giants in 1902. "Mugsy" had been a star infielder for the Baltimore Orioles during three-straight NL Pennant-winning seasons (1894-1896). In 1901, he became a player-manager for the new AL Baltimore Orioles (the original New York Yankees).

Christy Mathewson demonstrating a pitch.

McGraw's tendency to draw the wrath of AL umpires brought about his suspension from the strict new league. "Little Napoleon," as he was also known, retaliated by jumping to the Giants. He also brought several star players along with him. With the additions of "Iron Man" Joe McGinnity and Roger Bresnahan from Baltimore, the Giants won their third NL Championship in 1904.

The AL's Boston Pilgrims (the original Red Sox) beat the NL's Pittsburgh Pirates in the first "modern-day" World Series in 1903. The "Fall Classic" was canceled in 1904 when McGraw refused to let his players take the field. "Little Napoleon" was still at war with his former league. The next season, New York won the NL Pennant again. This time, McGraw would take his troops to battle.

Christy Mathewson shut out the AL's Philadelphia Athletics three times in the 1905 World Series. McGinnity tossed a fourth shutout as the Giants won their fourth World Championship.

Roger Bresnahan caught all four of the Giants' shutout victories. He was considered the greatest backstop of his day. Bresnahan was also responsible for introducing several improvements to the "tools of ignorance," including shin guards and padded face masks. In 1944, Roger Bresnahan became the first catcher inducted into the Baseball Hall of Fame.

In 1906, Joe McGinnity led the NL in wins (27) for the fifth time. He retired in 1908 after leading the "Senior Circuit" in shutouts (5) for the third time. "Iron Man" McGinnity was inducted into the Hall of Fame in 1946.

Richard "Rube" Marquard replaced "Iron Man" as a starting pitcher for the Giants in 1909. Marquard and Mathewson led New York to three more NL Pennants from 1911 to 1913. Each league championship was followed by defeat in the World Series. The three seasons were the best of Marquard's 18-year career. Rube Marquard entered the Hall of Fame in 1971.

John McGraw (center) at spring training with fellow Giants Bert Niehoff (left) and Ray Schalk (right).

Mugsy

While playing baseball in upstate New York, young John McGraw once broke some church windows with a long home run to right-center field. The incident brought about a beating from his father, who hated the game. The young McGraw protected himself from that day forward by learning to hit the ball to the opposite field. It was the beginning of a long career for Mugsy as baseball's greatest tactician.

Nothing was more important to John McGraw than winning baseball games. In his 31 seasons (1902-1932) as manager of the New York Giants, he led the team to 10 NL Pennants and 3 World Championships.

When New York plummeted to last place in 1915, McGraw decided it was time for some changes. Two years later, the Giants were NL Champions again. They were defeated in the 1917 World Series by the Chicago White Sox. It was the fourth-straight time New York had lost in the Fall Classic.

By the time the Giants returned to the World Series in 1921, baseball was becoming more of an offensive game. The man most responsible for the change played his home games at New York's Polo Grounds. But he was not a Giant. His name was Babe Ruth. The "Bambino's" home run power led the New York Yankees to their first AL Pennant. They faced their landlords, the New York Giants, in the first World Series to be played in a single ballpark.

First baseman George Kelly steps up to the plate.

The Giants defeated the Yankees in the best-of-nine-game series (5-3) to win their fifth World Championship. Mugsy's new roster included Hall-of-Famers at four positions. George "Highpockets" Kelly (1B), Frankie Frisch (3B), Dave "Beauty" Bancroft (SS), and Ross "Pep" Youngs (OF) would remain together through four-straight NL Pennant-winning seasons (1921-1924).

Frisch was traded to the St. Louis Cardinals after the 1926 season for the great Rogers Hornsby. Frankie would go on to become the player-manager for St. Louis' infamous "Gashouse Gang" (1934). Hornsby, another Hall-of-Famer, played only one season in New York.

In the 1922 World Series, the Giants defeated the Yankees for the second-straight time. Yankee Stadium was completed in 1923, and the "Bronx Bombers" returned to meet the Giants in the Fall Classic for the third-straight time. The Yankees recorded their first of a record 23 World Championships in six games (4-2). The Washington Senators defeated the Giants in the 1924 World Series (4-3), as New York's four-year run of NL Championships came to an end.

Casey Stengel, who managed more world champions (seven) than any man in history, played for Little Napoleon in New York. Upon the introduction of the batting helmet, Stengel said of his former manager, "If we'd had them when I was playing, John McGraw would have insisted that we go up to the plate and get hit in the head."

Nothing was more important to Mugsy than winning baseball games. Little Napoleon retired in 1932. He died of cancer less than two years later, February 25, 1934. John McGraw was inducted into the Baseball Hall of Fame in 1937.

Legacy

In 1923, John McGraw personally convinced Bill Terry to give up a career in the oil business for one in baseball. "Memphis Bill" became an outstanding defensive first baseman, and won the 1930 NL Batting Crown (.401). Two years later, Terry replaced "Little Napoleon" as manager of the Giants.

Mel Ott came to New York in 1926. He was 17 years old. At 5-feet, 9-inches tall, "Master Melvin" was not a giant in stature. Kicking his right leg high in the air, the left-handed slugger generated enough power to lead the NL in home runs six times. When he was 20 years old, Ott also became the youngest player to blast 40 home runs in a single season (42). By age 36, Ott had made 11-straight All-Star appearances, and was the NL's all-time home run king (511).

Carl Hubbell was the Giants' "King of the Hill." His career was also rescued by John McGraw. Hubbell developed a pitch called the "screwball," which he was forbidden from throwing while in the Detroit Tigers' minor league system. McGraw noticed that the pitch resembled the backwards-breaking "fadeaway" of Christy

Facing page: Giants' slugger Mel Ott.
Right: Ott belts one out of the ballpark.

Mathewson. He signed Hubbell to the Giants in 1928, and encouraged him to use the pitch. In the 1934 All-Star Game, "King Carl" struck out five-straight Hall-of-Famers. Babe Ruth, Lou Gehrig, Jimmie Foxx, Al Simmons, and Joe Cronin were each victimized by Hubbell's patented new pitch!

Memphis Bill, Master Melvin, and King Carl carried Mugsy McGraw's legacy to three NL Pennants in the 1930s. Hubbell led the league in wins (23) and ERA (1.66) in 1933, and became the first Giant to win the NL Most Valuable Player (MVP) Award. New York captured its 13th NL Pennant! In the World Series, King Carl pitched 20 innings against the Washington Senators without allowing an earned run. Mel Ott's solo homer in the 9th inning of Game 5 capped the New York Giants' 1933 World Championship.

The Giants returned to the Fall Classic in 1936 and 1937. Each time they were defeated by their cross-town rivals, the New York Yankees. Carl Hubbell won his second NL MVP Award in 1936 after leading the league in wins (26) and ERA (2.31) for the second time in four seasons. King Carl posted his fifth-straight 20-win season in 1937 (22) to lead the league for the third time.

"Memphis Bill" Terry played his last game in 1936. He continued to manage the team until handing the job over to Mel Ott in 1942. Terry is the most recent player in NL history to post a single-season batting average above the .400 mark. His .341 lifetime batting average is among the highest in the history of the game. Bill Terry was inducted into the Baseball Hall of Fame in 1954. He was preceded by "Master Melvin" Ott (inducted in 1951) and "King Carl" Hubbell (inducted in 1947).

Carl Hubbell in 1937 during spring training in Havana, Cuba.

Nice Guys

Mel Ott was one of the New York Giants' most popular players. The right field bleachers at the Polo Grounds were nicknamed "Ottville," for all of the long drives he deposited there. As manager, however, Ott failed to bring New York an NL Pennant.

According to Leo Durocher, Master Melvin was too nice. In 1946, Durocher was managing the Brooklyn Dodgers. While speaking to a group of reporters about Ott and the Giants, Durocher uttered his most famous words. "Take a look at that Number 4 there," he said. "A nicer guy never drew breath. Take a look at them. All nice guys. They'll finish last. *Nice guys finish last!"*

Durocher's words proved to be both memorable and prophetic. The New York Giants finished last in 1946 for only the fifth time in their long and storied history. What Durocher could not have known was that he would leave his job in Brooklyn to replace Mel Ott two years later. For Dodger fans, it was the ultimate betrayal. For the Giants, it signaled a return to glory.

The New York Giants' 1951 season came to be known as "The Little Miracle of Coogan's Bluff," after the site upon which the Polo Grounds was built. What was miraculous was the Giants' stretch-drive, in which they won 37 of their final 44 ball games, and tied the Brooklyn Dodgers on the final day of the season.

A three-game playoff was set up to determine the NL Championship. After splitting the first two games, the Giants and Dodgers played the decisive contest on a gloomy day at New York's Polo Grounds. Brooklyn held a 4-1 lead when the Giants began their 9th-inning rally. With one run in and two runners on, the Dodgers called on Ralph Branca to put out the fire. Bobby Thomson's "Shot Heard 'Round the World" made the Giants the 1951 NL Champions!

San Francisco

Christy Mathewson pitched 17 seasons for the Giants, winning more games (373) than any pitcher in NL history.

From 1902-1932, manager John "Mugsy" McGraw led the Giants to 10 NL Pennants and 3 World Championships.

George "Highpockets" Kelly was inducted into the Baseball Hall of Fame in 1973.

Hall-of-Famer Mel Ott started with the Giants at the age of 17.

Giants

In 1933, "King Carl" Hubbell was the first Giant to win the NL MVP.

Willie Mays was the 1951 Rookie of the Year. During his major league career, he hit 660 home runs, third best in history.

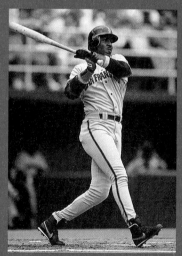

Willie "Stretch" McCovey was named the 1959 NL Rookie of the Year.

While with the Giants in 1993, Barry Bonds won his third NL MVP Award.

The next day, the Giants carried their momentum to a victory over the New York Yankees in Game 1 of the World Series. In the end, the "Bronx Bombers" proved too powerful to overcome, however, defeating the Giants in six games (4-2).

Willie Mays was the 1951 NL Rookie of the Year. In 1952, he was called to serve the U.S. Army during the Korean War. With Mays gone from the Giants' lineup, the Brooklyn Dodgers won NL Pennants in 1952 and 1953. They were defeated by the Yankees in the World Series both years. Baseball in New York was at its peak.

In 1954, Willie Mays returned to New York and won the NL Batting Crown (.345) and MVP Award. The Giants won their last NL Pennant in the Big Apple. In Game 1 of the World Series against the Cleveland Indians, Mays raced to the deepest part of the Polo Grounds to chase down a 425-foot blast off the bat of Vic Wertz. Willie's over-the-shoulder catch robbed Cleveland of a scoring opportunity, and gave a national television audience a chance to see the greatest center fielder of all time.

Mays had become a hometown hero in New York. During his off days, he frequently played stickball with kids in the streets of Harlem. His characteristic greeting, "Say Hey," became a lasting nickname. The Giants swept the Indians (4-0) in the 1954 World Series to become World Champions for the eighth time—proving to everyone that nice guys can also finish first!

Willie Mays slides safely into home.

Willie McCovey hit two home runs during the 1969 All-Star Game.

San Francisco, "Say Hey!"

New York City was the birthplace of baseball. From 1949 through 1956, the Big Apple was home to eight-straight World Championship teams. The New York Giants (2), Brooklyn Dodgers (5) and New York Yankees (7) won 14 of the 16 AL and NL Pennants during those years. In 1958, the Giants and Dodgers moved West to "the Land of Opportunity" in California.

The San Francisco Giants played their first two seasons in Seals Stadium before Candlestick Park was completed in 1960. Orlando "Baby Bull" Cepeda (1958) and Willie "Stretch" McCovey (1959)—each named NL Rookie of the Year—joined Willie "Say Hey" Mays in those years. The three would combine for five-straight NL home run titles in the early 1960s, despite the negative weather conditions that prevailed at "the Stick."

In 1962, the San Francisco Giants won 16 of their final 19 games to catch the first-place Los Angeles Dodgers on the last day of the season. In a playoff to decide the NL Championship, the Giants defeated the Dodgers in three games (2-1). Then they faced the New York Yankees in the 1962 World Series.

The Series came down to the final out of Game 7. The Yankees were clinging to a slim 1-0 lead when Mays doubled, sending Matty Alou to third base. Willie McCovey stepped up and lined a bullet that was snared by New York's second baseman Bobby Richardson. Once again, the Yankees were World Champions.

San Francisco would have to wait 27 years before returning to the Fall Classic. They closed the 1960s with five-straight second-place finishes. In the third year of divisional play, the Giants won their first NL West Division Title. They were defeated in the 1971 NLCS (National League Championship Series) by the Pittsburgh Pirates.

Juan Marichal was San Francisco's leading pitcher through all of the team's near-miss seasons. Marichal made the first of his nine All-Star appearances in 1962. His unique windup was likened to a cobra uncoiling. With 243 career wins and a 2.89 lifetime ERA, Juan Marichal was inducted into the Hall of Fame in 1983.

Willie Mays played 21 seasons in the Giants' outfield. He was an NL All-Star 20 consecutive times (1954-1973). By 1966, Mays had surpassed Mel Ott as the NL's all-time home run king. In 1972, Mays was traded to the New York Mets so he could finish his career in the city where it began. His final at-bat came in the 1973 World Series. It was a game-winning RBI single.

In the history of Major League Baseball, only Henry Aaron (755) and Babe Ruth (714) have hit more home runs than Willie Mays (660). Defensively, the "Say Hey Kid" is without equal. He holds the all-time record for putouts (7,095) by an outfielder, and won 12-straight Gold Glove Awards from 1957 to 1968. (Prior to 1957, the honor did not exist.) He is the standard upon which great all-around players are measured. Willie Mays was inducted into the Baseball Hall of Fame in 1979.

Willie Mays (left) and pitcher Juan Marichal (right) in the locker
room after the 1964 All-Star Game.

Barry Bonds gets a hit during a game against the San Diego Padres.

Socks And Bonds

In his final seasons with San Francisco, Willie Mays befriended a young teammate named Bobby Bonds. In 1969, Bonds followed Mays, becoming the second player in major league history to reach 30 home runs and 30 stolen bases in a single season. He would go on to reach the 30-30 plateau 5 times in his career. To further secure the relationship, Willie Mays became the godfather to Bonds' young son, Barry.

Willie McCovey returned to the Giants in 1977 after spending three seasons with the San Diego Padres. "Stretch" passed Mel Ott in 1979 for the most home runs by a lefthander in NL history (521). Willie was a fan favorite in San Francisco, just as "Master Melvin" had been in New York. Willie McCovey was inducted into the Hall of Fame in 1986.

San Francisco won its second NL West Division Title in 1987. The team was defeated in the NLCS by the St. Louis Cardinals. Two years later, San Francisco won its second NL Pennant. The 1989 Giants featured a lineup of sluggers who nicknamed themselves the "Pacific Sock Exchange."

Kevin Mitchell provided most of the sock, leading the NL in home runs (47) and RBIs (125). Mitchell's performance earned him the 1989 NL MVP Award. Will "The Thrill" Clark (.333) finished just behind San Diego's Tony Gwynn (.336) in the race for the NL Batting Crown. Third baseman Matt Williams was brought up from the minor leagues at midseason, completing the Giants' powerful portfolio. Williams knocked out 18 home runs in 84 games, and combined with first baseman Clark to give San Francisco solid defense at the corner positions.

The Giants outslugged the Chicago Cubs in the 1989 NLCS, as the "Sock Exchange" continued to furnish long-ball dividends. In the World Series, their home-run market came crashing down along with the Bay Bridge, which connects San Francisco with Oakland. The Oakland Athletics swept the Giants (4-0) in a Fall Classic that was delayed 10 days by a devastating earthquake. Just as Game 3 was about to get underway, Candlestick Park began to shake from a tremor measuring 7.1 on the Richter Scale. Sixty-seven people around the San Francisco-Oakland Bay Area lost their lives in the disaster.

Barry Bonds followed his seismic lineage to the major leagues in 1986. While playing for the Pittsburgh Pirates, Barry wore number 24 on his uniform in honor of his godfather, Willie Mays. After winning the NL MVP Award twice (1990 and 1992) for the Pirates, Bonds joined the Giants in 1993. San Francisco finished with the second-best record in baseball (103-59) that season, but finished one game behind the Atlanta Braves (104-58) in the race for the NL West Division Title. Barry Bonds was named the NL MVP for the third time.

Facing page: Chili Davis (right) is congratulated at home plate by teammate Candy Maldonado (left) after Davis scored both men on a two-run homer during a game against the Cincinnati Reds.

In Search Of A Title

In 1996, Osvaldo Fernandez became a Giant. The Cuban-born pitching sensation joins Barry Bonds and Matt Williams as San Francisco continues to search for its first World Championship. It is said that baseball can break your heart. After nearly 40 years by the Bay, the Giants may have left their hearts in New York City.

The San Francisco Giants have never won a World Championship. Since moving to the Bay Area, the team has survived the swirling winds of Candlestick Park, several attempts to uproot the franchise, and even a World Series earthquake! With more than a century of history and generations of great players behind them, the Giants continue to invest in the future, hoping to recreate the glory days of Gotham in the city by the Golden Gate.

Glossary

All-Star: A player who is voted by fans as the best player at one position in a given year.

American League (AL): An association of baseball teams formed in 1900 which make up one-half of the major leagues.

American League Championship Series (ALCS): A best-of-seven-game playoff with the winner going to the World Series to face the National League Champions.

Batting Average: A baseball statistic calculated by dividing a batter's hits by the number of times at bat.

Earned Run Average (ERA): A baseball statistic which calculates the average number of runs a pitcher gives up per nine innings of work.

Fielding Average: A baseball statistic which calculates a fielder's success rate based on the number of chances the player has to record an out.

Hall of Fame: A memorial for the greatest baseball players of all time, located in Cooperstown, New York.

Home Run (HR): A play in baseball where a batter hits the ball over the outfield fence scoring everyone on base as well as the batter.

Major Leagues: The highest ranking associations of professional baseball teams in the world, currently consisting of the American and National Baseball Leagues.

Minor Leagues: A system of professional baseball leagues at levels below Major League Baseball.

National League (NL): An association of baseball teams formed in 1876 which make up one-half of the major leagues.

National League Championship Series (NLCS): A best-of-seven-game playoff with the winner going to the World Series to face the American League Champions.

Pennant: A flag which symbolizes the championship of a professional baseball league.

Pitcher: The player on a baseball team who throws the ball for the batter to hit. The pitcher stands on a mound and pitches the ball toward the strike zone area above the plate.

Plate: The place on a baseball field where a player stands to bat. It is used to determine the width of the strike zone. Forming the point of the diamond-shaped field, it is the final goal a base runner must reach to score a run.

RBI: A baseball statistic standing for *runs batted in.* Players receive an RBI for each run that scores on their hits.

Rookie: A first-year player, especially in a professional sport.

Slugging Percentage: A statistic which points out a player's ability to hit for extra bases by taking the number of total bases hit and dividing it by the number of at bats.

Stolen Base: A play in baseball when a base runner advances to the next base while the pitcher is delivering the pitch.

Strikeout: A play in baseball when a batter is called out for failing to put the ball in play after the pitcher has delivered three strikes.

Triple Crown: A rare accomplishment when a single player finishes a season leading their league in batting average, home runs, and RBIs. A pitcher can win a Triple Crown by leading the league in wins, ERA, and strikeouts.

Walk: A play in baseball when a batter receives four pitches out of the strike zone and is allowed to go to first base.

World Series: The championship of Major League Baseball played since 1903 between the pennant winners from the American and National Leagues.

Index